James Rothstein

A Syndrome of Global Anarchy

After globalization,global popular anarchy

Economic sydtems of popular shareholding corporations

Popular justice by anarchist groups

The new age after World War 3 is global anarchy

Atheism and the belief in logic

The model of anarchy in Haiti

The end of militarism in the new anarchy age

The model of anarchy in Spain

None will say where he is from

International peace and the quest for tranquility

Customary laws of anarchy

A global revolution must start to free all the citizen of the world from the perils of wars and suppression.Popular anarchy will be a reality with this global revolution

After global revolution we will live in the new age.International peace and prosperity .Freedom and justice will become a reality with the actions of anarchist groups.Communities of people will coexist and will be engaged in continuous dialogue to solve any difference.Freedom of expression and equality for all.Equal rights and privileges will become customary laws and only customs will exist and will guide citizens and their behavior.Justice by the people and for the benefit of the people.Political systems will be erased and dissolved .

Militarism will end in all parts of the world.

Money from medium and big corporations will be shared to everyone and everyone will have equal income.Atheism will the major belief.Atheism means the belief in scientific knowledge and rationality.

Fantasy and imagination will be the way of thinking in the future.Tranquility of the mind.

After the current war a global revolution will start that will establish a de facto international system of anarchy.Noone will say where he is from and all the wars will end forever.

Now is the significant historical moment to start the revolution of anarchists.

All nations will be so tired by this war that they will seek a new system.They will seek peace.After this global crisis all nations will choose a political system similar to that of Spain and Haiti and we must use these nations and their community systems of organization as models to build similar models in other nations and we must mimick the two nations.

We will see the end of nationalism and the dawn of a new global system of Ordo Ab Chaos.Order through chaos.When we establish global chaos with wars and revolutions ,we establish in the end global peace and global freedom for all.

A Matter of Mass

The end of the Bible,the end of religions and atheism

The practical value of mathematical logic in decision making

The clash of religions and the end of mankind

Mathematical foundations of philosophy and the explanation of the nature of mass

The mud peoples

2

A scenario of World War 3

$M = E \times L \div P(\exp(c \times e)) \times \ln(P)$

M=mass, E=energy, L=light,

P=perception, exp=exponential function,

c=cosmic radiation, e=electricity

ln=lognumber, P=optical nerve×brainpower

Mass is a function of its derivatives as a perpetuation of its quadratic forms and hyperforms.God died in the sixties so don't believe in God.We live the end of the bible and the begining of global atheism.World war 3 started in Syria and will end in Ukraine,Taiwan and Pakistan.Nato will invade many nations to bring peace.The artillery

3

will bomb sporadically and spontaneously.The oil refineries of the enemies will be destroyed with sabotage operations from the Black Ops.The nuclear capabilities of the enemy nations will be destroyed also with sabotage.Then Nato will bomb from the air and at the same time with parallel processing it will launch nuclear missiles against the perpetrators of humanity.This will happen because the enemies will have no air defence.The mightiest power on air allways wins modern wars.The enemy will have no capability to retaliate with nuclear missiles and will surrender when it sees the Nato stealth bombers.To win a war a nation needs bigger mass and many times the mass is a matter of perception,brainpower and aesthetic

4

manipulation of soft power.Modern wars since World war 2 end with nuclear bombings and the same thing will happen in this war.We have to use game theory and scenario planning to plan this war.When the e lose their oil refineries and oil wells we can negotiate with them from a position of advantage and we can say to them to disarm peacefully or we will not let them buy oil from Saudi Arabia which is an ally of USA.

This a war free capitalism against the political religion of communism on the other side. The biggest danger for America is a nuclear retaliation from its enemies and the Black Ops have to cancel this option for the enemies of mankind. This is a war of logic versus irrationality, of humanism versus intolerance for differences. We have

5

to win this war because we are better than our enemies and mathematical logic dictates that the good wins to rebuild and evolve the earth.

Critic on Malthus

Evil Literature

The most evil text ever written by human hands.

The text that reveals who the Antichrist really is.

By Karl Lever

2

3˙

The Antichrist is the embodiment of human lies.Zero and existence.The is and the is not.Image and mirror.This book is written by myself under the influence of a satanic spirit called Black Angel. Zero and existence.The is and the is not.Image and mirror.This book is written by myself under the influence of a satanic spirit called Black Angel.There are two hypotheses about the birth of this evil spirit which manifests itself as a Black God ,mean and aggressive.The first is I created it from my subconscious a night I was having sex with a butterfly so beautifull that the evolution of this mind started a new age of fantastic numbers existential Lucifer who also appeared to me as a red God made of nuclear energy.The second hypothesis that sounds closer to the truth than

4

the first is that the Black Angel revealed his form and character to me and to no one else the same exact moment my testosterone was very high from a wild night of sex with sexually overactive pop music dancers.

With tight bodies.

The Satanists appeared first and they said to me,the secret name of Satan is BLACK ANGEL.

When I call him he will come.But I asked the same Satanists afterwords and they said that they never thought that name for my God.

This is the first revelation of the Black Angel

5

And I will describe his character in full extend.He is very mean very sexual and talks like an evil demon.He possesses my brain from time to time and he always lives inside my brain and I control his behavior .He knows all the secrets of mankind and all the secrets of the demons and he explained to me many hidden laws of the universe and many hidden rules of thumb that I can use to make my self understood by the inferior races.Because he will come in the future to reign on Earth.He already exist

6

s in my brain and the sexual tention helps the creation of these spirits which come from the vast literature of demonology and they appear to men of wisdom.He likes to beat people and have sex but I allways control him.

The dialectics have been evolved into the post modern mirror of illusions.As the matter and antimatter,as the gravity and antigravity of stealth bombers rule the planet by the fear of nuclear holocausts.Time existed before the creation of the universe.If we can see the icon of preexisting

time we can and I did so,invent
VIRTUAL MATHEMATICS.

Like the imaginary numbers develop
themselves into 8 dimensions as the
cube has eight narrow points.The
cube is the perfect shape as it can
evolve by mating with other oblects or

7

transform with the power of the
fantasy of the mathematician into the
perfect six narrow points,the so called
Star of David.The mathematical
equations exist into the brain
unformed,untouched,undiscovered.B
ecause the elements are numberless
and the negative numbers expand
into numberless variations and
directions.But let's discuss the issue of
eight dimensional space ,because I
believe the understanding of this

space will let us discover new ways to solve problems with complex numbers.

They decided to kill the big god by inventing new younger and more youthfull ones.Am I Deranged? But the time come again and again when I wonder in my freaky dreams if I am an animal with a psyche.God is many

8

animals combined with electrolysis ,with sperm from many older gods and an aristocratic genealogy from the kings of Egyptian animal gods with many female eggs inside one womb.The hawk is the bringer of war.It means We Kill You.The bat brings radar or sonar activity and understanding.The Scorpio is immortal,the crow as well.The tragedy of being a God is to have no one similar to you to have no friends.And my brain is hard enough the human fallacies but animal enough to recognize the inferiority of descedants of apes.Who is the most chaotic thinker will surely win the lottery of Fibbonacci numbers.God has no friends no lovers,he only rapes to reprocude his kind,even if they are uncontrollable and experimental as

9

God himself is uncontrollable and experimental.They created him without knowing everything in advance of races and species weird like the dark water that runs inside the veins of lizards and evil scorpios who run to kill the opponent.It is a strange phenomenon the curbes ofemotional disturbances in the shadow government that we want to establish to run the planet.The resources the animal kingdom, the clones, everything.It is madness to be happy all the time.Overkill.Our goal in life is to prove the superiority of our DNA helix.From the bottomless pit of hell the devil cries and we had an orgy with him last night to prove we signed with blood but others people's blood the contracts of success.The vanity fair of emotional decadence,but gods

10

are not robots and they compete against other gods and demons and angels in an never ending game.

I have one hundred fathers and many of them are gods and many of them are reptiles and many of them are not even humans.So I do not have an established pattern of behavior amodel to imitate,so I have to kill all the time to survive,because this is the animal kingdom and it is the survival of the fittest and the evolution of mankind under the content of nazi death camps and secret experiment of eugenics.I have two mothers so who raised me?The tragedy of Gods ,They have noone similar to them.Gods are orphans many followers but it's lonely at the top.I trust my killer instinct.After all we have the ANTICHRIST in front of us.And the

11

retard priests of weak gods have to perish and die under the heavy hand of strong gods.They designed my being ,my existence.My fate is to run the global government and many secret cabals,like the Bilderberg

Group and the illuminati support me
to reign but I have also many enemies.

12

The Decadanse of Peacefull Societies

Peace means the end of life .Only with
natural death does the living animal
find nirvana which means non
existence and it is a dangerous
religious point of view as it is
antilife.Humanity evolves with mixed
breeding and blood
transactions.Hybrids and The Angel of
Death really exist.He revealed his
name to me and this is Black
Angel.Call him and he will appear in
front of you and he will say.You called
me many times and now you see me
in front of you.I am real I have many
kids but you are my real son.

I am the violent entrepreneur.The hero of yesterday was a psychopath.The evil spirit speaks from within and he calls himself The Black angel.

13

Madness and the metropolis.

Out of the mad mob labyrinth of yesterdays,comes and derives the flower of todays evil.It is the kaleidoscope of multiculture society of the ladies of socialites as they are called and they polute the essence of human intervention all the way from the street to the luxurious apartments of high decadanse.

The average human experiences life in Gotham city or the metropolis as traumatic and criminally dangerous.Life in Gotham is a gamble where the innocent bourgoise hang around the square of mediocracy and never bother to look to the other side of hell.

14

The obvious is unexpected and rather oblivious to the corners of someones' eyes where the tears and depression evolve into everyday behavior.

Spiritualism

We can invoke spirits to cooperate with us and to be our guides to give us strength.A spirited man is a man who talks with spirits it is as easy as that.Call them and they will appear in front of you as images from the spiritual world.To the selected one in time of intense body activity the demon will appear to protect the individual.

He will say his secret name the one
the individual can use to call
him.Human beings must have spirits
to guide them.Spirits live inside the

15

brain.He is very powerfull and
viscious.

He gets excited with sex and other
kinds of gymnastics as I explained
before.

The strange bulldog of Mrs Degilvy
and the one thousand canaries of Mr
Strangecraft

He talks,he talks,yelled
unnexpectangly Mrs Degilvy looking at
the dog.The dna of the dog had
changed due to a blood transfusion.It
started t say tales of old navy men.The
secret name of the devil is Black

Angel.The doctor of neurosurgery Mr Strangecraft appeals to the idea of

16

heavy melodic musical that emerges from the thousand of canaries that sing in his backyard.Mr Strangecraft is an odd being acting responsibly to the responsible and irresponsibly to the irresponsible.Give your love to the mean people because they deserve it.Love should be wasted to mediocrities of average convictions and average passions.Thousands of canaries fly and sing beautifull songs at the Canary Islands.

How the Antichrist has to behave.

He has to do politainment.To entertain and do politics at the same time.Live killings live death on television ,orgies and criminal psychology on live news

17

networks.Men and lions live in the same body.The mixer of blood.The vampire .

Drinks the blood of healthy individuals and healthy daughters of overkill.

The Satanic Talmud is the application of Talmudic rules to Satanists and their lives.

The evil eye is a diatribe on hate.

I hate with meter.I think therefore I hate.A natural consequence of my wisdom.Tere is no our there is what is mine. I will expose all the destructive paranoia collective genius.The presence of hyperego.We are the cult of black Saturday.We are the villains of the continent.I support the middle solution.This is my philosophical

18

thesis.The cultivated self-knowledge of my essential existence.I do not support the golden solution or the perfect solution because the mathematical type ,the equation of its finding is impossible to codify,to be algorithmically conceived in its extreme limits and fields.The deductive analysis explain that I support the middle solution which is the optimal according to the statistical method of Monte Carlo and the stochastic processes Cauchy.Alber Camy said in his infamous work the nights of Caligula that the middle path is the stratagem of Roman emperors and concubines of Pompey.Who walked on the abnormal road in the

center and not on the hidden oath
and loath of extremisms from both
sides.This is path dependence.The

19

birds of the night live forever.The wise
man is looking for the defects of other
men.He uses philosophical induction
analysis so that the first theorem
leads to the second and the
third.Freedom is the highest principle
of the wise man.Descartes said I think
therefore I am.The evolutionary
thinking of this theorem explains itself
in Homers' Iliad with its lessons for
life.All the young people should read
Iliad and Odyssey of Homer to learn
how to live their lives.They can use
the patterns of history and ancient
stories not only to predict the future
but to influence the outcome.I what
but what do I think.I think of hate,like

all humans.I hate therefore I am.i
think therefore I have freedom.

This is the core the wisdom of wise
men.This is the secret of their victory

20

and their successes in life.I think
therefore I am free and I hate so I am
free.This is the highest wisdom.The
thesis of philosophy of I hate
therefore I am is based on the
observation that to fight and signal
toughness and meaness,means
survival and victory.The characteristic
of Homeric heroes and ancient Greek
royals is their fight and their violence.I
am mean and aggressive therefore I
am.I fight all the time continuously
and I signal criminal behavior
therefore I am.It is a thesis of criminal
philosophy of the mass culture for the

selected that will lead the masses and the revolutionary man to the new dawn and the Aquarian age of freedom and prosperity for all.Authenticity and originality are the principles of victorious men.A first

21

consideration of international politics that appears as a futuristic theorem and theoretical model is the collusion between the superpowers of the West and the East.A fulfilledand self-fullfilling prophecy was that they will cooperate in an arrangement of coopetition to divide the global market and customers to share the profits and to bring international peace.Nations will allways drive themselves to wars from all the directions of the horizon.The cycles of hot and cold wars,clashes of armies will continue until the end of humanity.Until the last two humans on earth kill each other,they will perish and vanish.This is human nature.Violence and aggressiveness,hostility and killing.Persons make

22

history,personalities decide the outcome of politics,defence and global affairs,outcomes like wars.Not historical forces which a false belief.In this arrangement of collusion between superpowers to avoid the perils of human extinction,the West and the East,their leading nations will bring peace among them and peripheral wars which they will both agree about.Wars drive their economies with the defence budget,technological research relating to war and spending,creation of new money to finance the war with the purpose to acquire natural resources which are scarce and their exploitation will pay for the interest of loans to the government.War is business and money will allways drive the minds of men who make

23

important decisions.The population bombs of the Third world will force the mids of decision makers from the two superpowers to downsize these populations.They will sacrifice the criminal nations,the few for the benefit of leaders and master races.The idea of masters and servants in a civilized manner of the twenty first century will allways exist.The purpose of wars will also be the reduction of size and weaken the enemies of arts,letters and modern culture.What this thesis calls the ne aquarian age is this design in global politics and the future who want to know and learn.The aquarian age is a concept of mass culture of an astrological philosophy and this subject I will examine in a future essay.Malthus knew the designs of

24

leaders of nations and the mechanism of the movement and pogroms of populations who are unwanted because they are poor and they suffer in their poverty and they allways start a struggle of clashes.

Tribal Wars and Global Decadanse

The end of humanity seems now possible because of global tribal wars .Interdependence between nations makes war easy to the man who has knowledge of the mechanism of global politics.Global decay is now visible because of long lasting and continuous wars.Atheism now will be the religion or the end of all religions and the birth of mathematical logic that will replace all religions as a form of thought and a form of culture.In the present time we don't have a clash of civilizations but a war among tribes,we see wars and beefs between cities often between neibghehoods that will lead to urban warfare of

2

global scale.Mutually assured destruction is an idea that will be visible if the war in Ukraine continues and if we are not carefull.This scenario of the Cold war may be a reality in the future.The post apocalyptic world of Mad Max may become a reality in many regions of the earth.Due to nuclear catastrophe.To win the war in Ukraine, Nato has to bomb with the artillery the military camps of the enemy to frighten them.Then we have to destroy with air bombings and covert operations the Ukrainian oil wells and oil refineries.Nato must have its own navy base in the western coast of Ukraine in the Black Sea in order to invade Ukraine from the sea.A multiethnic force is necessary so that many nations accept responsibility for the invasion and the

3

reason for this operation will be to
save the Ukrainians from genocide by
the Russian army.Nato will probably
be able to hold the border in a vertical
line in the middle of Ukraine,because
the eastern part of the country is
heavily populated with a Russian
minority.If we cut off the oil supply of
the Rusian army and the Russian navy
then they will lose the capability to
move their army and they will stand
still.Nato forces have to control the
military air bases in Ukraine.Russia
will start or has already started a
genocide in Ukraine and it behaves
like Serbia against Albanians.Nato in a
few years will have the alibi to bomb
Russia with nuclear weapons to stop
this genocide against Ukrainian

population.Then Nato will win the war.Pakistan has started an

4

infiltration inside Chinese and Indian territory and my prediction is they will start a war against India.Then India will win the war because of larger nuclear missiles buildup.Then USA willbomb India to reduce its population and to stop the war.The oil rich countries of Islamic faith will friends with USA,which is an important thing for America because of it's oil dependence and because of limited use of renewable energy source and green energy.The American navy protects the straits of Taiwan but if it moves away from the Chinese sea space China will invade Taiwan.Then USA will an alibi to bomb China with enriched plutonium bombs and nuclear intercontinental missiles to stop the genocide in Taiwan.The populations of the third world nations

5

have to be minimized because they are a big problem for the West.They consume a lot of oil and they are a threat for the Western civilization.After the war we will see the dawn of a new world order.Earth is able to hold only half a billion people.All the rest will probably die in a global nuclear holocaust.The Western civilization has to survive this war and build a better future for our youth and for everyone else.USA has to cancel the nuclear capability of Russia,China and India and then destroy them with intercontinental nuclear missiles because in a few years with all the wars these nations

started USA will have the alibi to
destroy them.All the soldiers of the
great American nation will unite to

6

end this genocide of Asia against
Europe and to save the hobbits.